THE READ AND WRITE SERIES: Book 3

My Crazy Dog:
My Narrative Essay

By Darcy Pattison

Illustrations by
Ewa O'Neill

Other Mims House Books
MimsHouse.com

Wisdom, the Midway Albatross: Surviving the Japanese Tsunami and other Disaster for Over 60 Years (nonfiction picture book)
Starred PW review
2014-15 Sakura Medal Reading List – Children's book award from the English-speaking schools in Japan.

Abayomi, the Brazilian Puma: The True Story of an Orphaned Cub
 (nonfiction picture book)
2015 National Science Teacher's Association Outstanding Science Trade Book

Saucy and Bubba: A Hansel and Gretel Tale (novel)

The Girl, the Gypsy and the Gargoyle (novel)

Vagabonds: An American Fantasy (novel)

The Aliens, Inc. Chapter Book Series
> ***Kell, the Alien, Book 1***
> ***Kell and the Horse Apple Parade, Book 2***
> ***Kell and the Giants, Book 3***
> ***Kell and the Detectives, Book 4***

Read Other Books in The Read and Write Series

I Want a Dog: My Opinion Essay, Book 1
I Want a Cat: My Opinion Essay, Book 2

MimsHouse.com/newsletter
Get a free ebook - on us!

My Crazy Dog: My Narrative Essay

Published in the United States.
For permissions contact:
Mims House
1309 Broadway
Little Rock, AR 72202
USA
MimsHouse.com

Publisher's Cataloging-in-Publication data

Pattison, Darcy
My crazy dog: my narrative essay,
written by Darcy Pattison, illustrated by Ewa O'Neill
p. cm.
Includes teacher resource.
Paperback ISBN 978-1-62944-051-4
Hardcover ISBN 978-1-62944-052-1
eBook ISBN 978-1-62944-053-8

Summary: When Dennis's dog, Clark Kent, leads him on a chase, it becomes the perfect topic for a narrative essay
1. Dogs - Juvenile Fiction. 2. Essay - Juvenile Fiction. 3. Pets - Fiction.
I. O'Neill, Ewa, ill. II. Title.

PZ7. P238 My 2015
Library of Congress Control Number: 2015905857

CCSS.ELA-Literacy: W.K.3, W.K.7, W.1.3, W.1.7, W.2.3, W.2.7, W.3.3, W.3.4, W.3.5, W.3.6. W3.7 ; RL.K.1, RL.K.5, RL.K.7, RL.K.10, RL.1.1, RL.1.5, RL.1.7, RL.1.10, R.L2.1, RL2.5, RL2.7, RL 2.10, RL.3.1, RL.3.4, RL. 3.7, RL.3.9, RL.3.10, RL.4.1, RL.4.3, RL. 4.6, W.4.3, W.4.7. W.4.10.

A narrator tells stories, so a narrative essay tells about something that happened, real or imaginary.

Last month, my cousin Mellie and I each got a dog and a cat. Crazy things have happened since I got my dog, Clark Kent, and my cat, Barbie. Maybe I could tell about Clark Kent getting shots. I will try to remember about getting ready for the veterinarian.

See: hallway, baby's room
Hear: crying, barking, wah, woof, shhh
Smell: baby powder
Taste:
Feel:

Next, Clark ran outside.

See:
living room,
deck, curtains
Hear:
running on
carpet, swish
Smell:
wind from
outside
Taste:
Feel:

Swish!

Finally, he tried to hide under the porch.

See: eyes shining under porch
Hear: pant
Smell: wet fur, wet dirt, sweat
Taste:
Feel: wet, cool, slick fur

That's where I caught him and put his leash on him. We took Clark Kent to the vet and to get his shots.

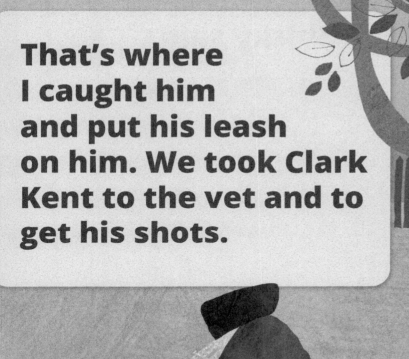

See: leash garden hose
Hear: click, water spraying
Smell: wet fur
Taste:
Feel: cold water

My Crazy Dog

"Clark Kent needs his shots," Mom said.

"Okay," I said. "I will get the leash."

When Clark Kent saw the leash, he ran.

First, Clark slid across the slick tile in the kitchen and slammed into Barbie's food bowl.

Crash! Clatter! Meow!

The cat food flipped up and into Mom's bowl of chocolate chip cookie dough.

Next, Clark clattered down the hallway.

"Come back!" I yelled.

"Shhh!" Mom said. "The baby is—"

"Woof! Woof! Woof!" said Clark.

"Wah! Wah!" cried baby Ruth.

Clark raced through the living room and straight for the door.

He's going to crash, I thought.

Instead, Clark burst through the curtain and out onto the deck.

Right away, Clark jumped at a blue bird. Squawk! Clark missed and fell against the bird feeder. Thunk!

Bravo!

Next, Clark raced to look at the orange goldfish in the pond. He fell in, and Clark Kent dripped water everywhere.

I chased him.

To get away, Clark leapt over the fish pond. Splash! His back legs landed in the pond. Now, he was wetter than ever.

Clark shook and shook. Then, I was wetter, too.

Finally, Clark Kent trotted under the porch. I thought if I walked up and hid the leash behind my back, he wouldn't run. Clark lay on the sandy dirt and panted. His fur was slick, muddy and smelly. It was cozy under the porch.

I pulled my dog into my lap, and we looked out at the puffy clouds in the sky. It had been a good chase.

From the doorway, Mom called, "We leave in ten minutes."

I hosed off Clark. Also I changed clothes. That's how we got Clark Kent to the vet's office on time.

At the vet's office, I let Clark Kent sit
in my lap so that the vet could look at him.
The vet gave Clark three shots.
I wanted to cry, but Clark didn't mind.
So that was OK.

WRITING NARRATIVE ESSAYS

A narrative essay tells a story. It can be about real or imagined experiences or events. Writing narrative essays means using strong sensory details, temporal words, connecting words, dialogue, thoughts and emotions.

Choosing a topic. Here are the guidelines for choosing a real event: the student must have been present and actively doing something; avoid events like car wrecks because the student is in a passive role; choose an everyday event; the event must take place within a 30 minute time period or less. For example, instead of an essay about a 3-day visit to a theme park, focus on the 30-minute wait and ride of the roller coaster.

Writing Stronger Details. Strong narratives use specific sensory details, or things you might see, hear, smell, taste, and feel. Feeling doesn't mean emotions; instead, think about things your hands would feel, like temperature and texture.

Temporal words. Use time words to keep the sequence of events in order: first, last, next, finally, then, at last, after, before, etc.

Connecting words and phrases. Use connecting words to show relationships among events: also, in addition, another, and, or, but, for example, because, etc.

Dialogue. Use the speech bubbles to help decide what goes inside the quotation marks.

Thoughts and emotions. Include thoughts and emotions to show what the character is thinking and feeling and the character's responses to a situation.

Introduction and conclusion. Establish the situation in the introduction. Provide a sense of closure at the end.

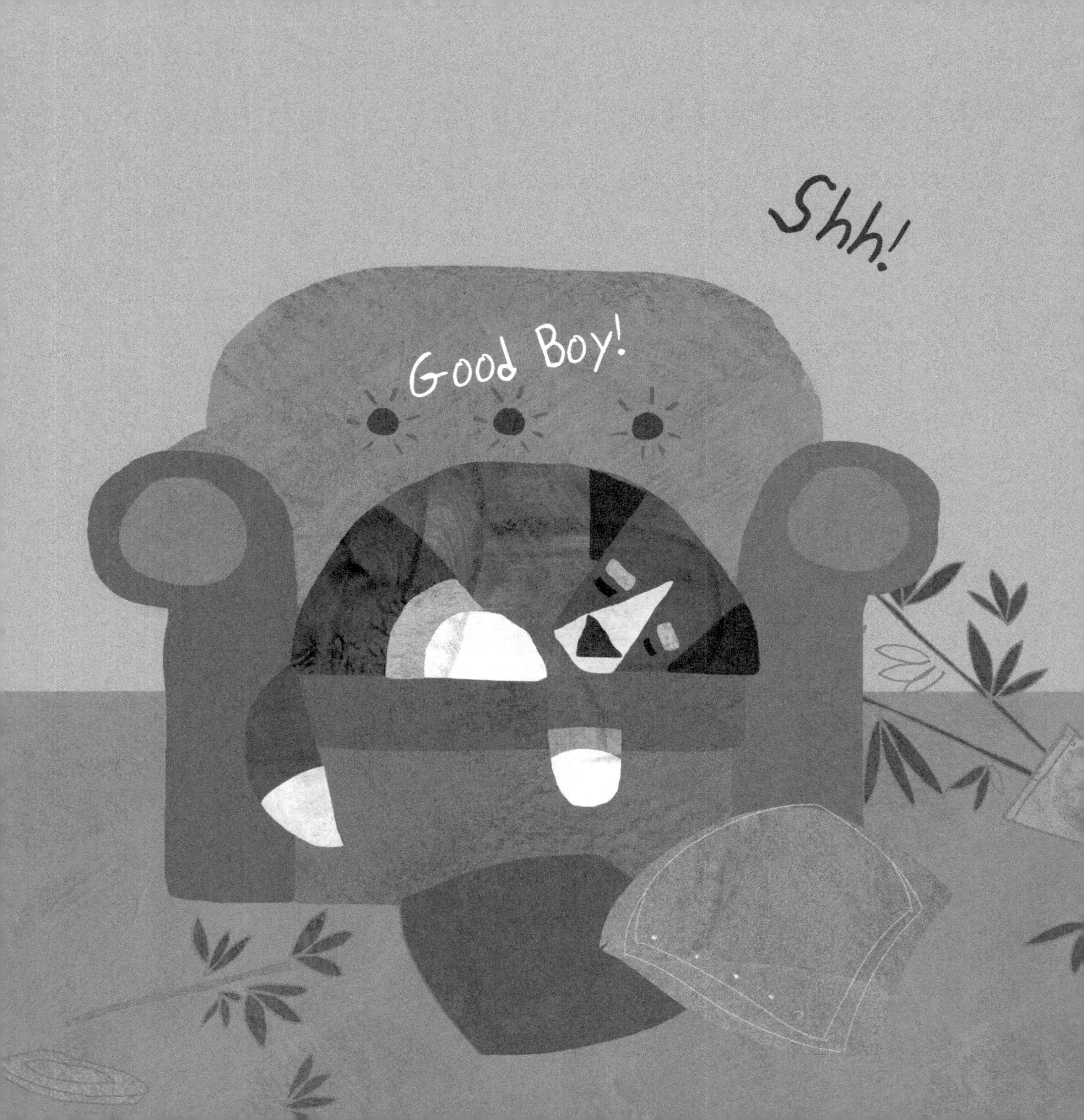
Shh!
Good Boy!

CPSIA information can be obtained
at www.ICGtesting.com
Printed in the USA
LVOW06*1044200217

524802LV00021B/166/P